Practical Christian Politics

By Glenn Sellnow

This book is dedicated to my former philosophy professors at Milwaukee School of Engineering. They probably thought I didn't learn anything meaningful during their classes because I am a poor student of philosophy but surprisingly I still remember some useful knowledge after forty years. MSOE is not known as a college dedicated to the pursuit of philosophy, but they did have a few related classes so I signed up for them because they looked like an easy way to earn some required humanities credits for my electrical engineering degree.

One of the philosophy professors had a particular dislike for my then-current flavor of Christianity and he found out that I was a Christian. He deliberately singled me out for some sarcastic insinuations regarding my beliefs which I simply tried to neutralize because I didn't have an ax to grind. I just wanted to collect my three humanities credits and graduate with a minimum of effort on my part.

Once he asked me if my Church would accept an alcoholic on the street and try to help the person with the implication being that we would consider ourselves too good. I responded without thinking and said, "Of course, we would even accept you." The rest of the student crowd was mildly amused by my response, and he didn't follow up on that line of attack. He reduced his number of insinuations after that incident, so I was able to coast through the rest of the class with relative ease which was my original goal.

Copyright

Table of Contents

Copyright

Table of Contents

Why Should Christians Be Political?

Benefits of Christian Politics

Prejudice Against Christians In Politics

Alternatives to Christian Involvement in Politics

Policy Changes Are Needed

Action Plan for Christian Politics

About the Author

Disclaimer

Social Media Help

Good News

Feedback and Reviews

"Do not place trust in princes,

in a son of humankind with whom there is no deliverance."

The Lexham English Bible (Ps 146:3)

Why Should Christians Be Political?

None of the major political parties in the United States are in perfect agreement with Christianity on all issues. The job of the Church is to save souls and not to become political. Why should Christians have anything to do with politics? Isn't it wrong for Christians to insert their religious beliefs into public policy?

I had a college friend who was a former South Vietnamese military officer. He had been in the South Vietnamese military before heavy American involvement and continued to fight even after the United States had abandoned Vietnam to the communists. Both of his parents had been killed by communists. His father's crime was that he was a teacher who taught contrary to communist doctrine and he also owned an orchard. Thuan (not his real name) was studying to be a lawyer in South Vietnam when he was forced to join the military. He saved the lives of many American and

Vietnamese soldiers as a helicopter pilot and aircraft commander.

I met Thuan at InterVarsity Christian Fellowship even though Thuan was not a Christian. I worked with Thuan on some group projects in college and we became good friends. He and his wife had recently visited us a few months ago when I found out that I had stage 4 cancer.

Think about what happened to Thuan and his home country. Atheistic communists murdered his parents and took over the government by violence. Communists did not take over the government peacefully in one day. "The Viet Cong are estimated to have killed about 36,725 South Vietnamese soldiers between 1957 and 1972. Statistics for 1968–72 suggest that "about 80 percent of the victims were ordinary civilians and only about 20 percent of them were government officials, policemen, members of the self-defense forces or pacification cadres." [1] Today the Vietnamese government claims there is freedom of religion in Vietnam but the reality is that you must bow your knee to communism before worshipping your God.

---

[1] Wikipedia: Lewy, Guenter (1980). *America in Vietnam*. Oxford University Press. p. 272-273. ISBN 9780199874231.

Could the United States become another Vietnam? Take a look at the nightly news in the year 2020 and tell me why it couldn't. Christians still have the legal right to speak their opinions publicly and to vote for the candidate of their choice but will these legal rights last much longer? Christian speech can be declared hate speech by law or the opinion of the media. Christian churches are not allowed to endorse candidates according to the Johnson amendment. Christian and others are afraid to publicly express their political views because of the media's political correctness and the real threat of violence. As I write this book, a black man was professionally executed in Milwaukee for his public support of an unpopular national political candidate. Christians say little about this situation because we have been muzzled by the majority's public opinion. Are we that timid and afraid? Do we want to hide our political opinions in our Church and hope no one bothers us?

The Nazi political party in Germany came to political power in 1932. Hitler was appointed Chancellor of Germany in 1933 and then created a one-party state. Hitler was appointed to power but could not have achieved that position without enough votes for his party to give him political strength. The Nazi party redefined basic Christian beliefs and opposed Christians that dared to object. Only pro-Nazi "christians" that accepted Nazi religious redefinition of basic Christian beliefs were allowed. The historical anti-Jewish writings of Martin Luther among other things were used to justify persecution and slaughter of the Jews. Christians in Germany could have voted against the Nazi party and stopped it from ever coming to power but most did not.

""Teacher, which commandment is greatest in the law?" And he said to him, " 'You shall love the Lord your God with all your heart and with all your soul and with all your mind.' This is the greatest and first commandment. And the second is like it: 'You shall love your neighbor as yourself.'"
The Lexham English Bible (Mt 22:36–39)

You can't "Love your neighbor as yourself" when you could have protected them from harm by the simple act of safely voting against pure evil. Every pastor and priest should have known what the Nazi party wanted and publicly denounced it to their congregations but most of them compromised with the Nazis. They either agreed with evil or were too afraid to say anything. Vocal dissidents met with violence from the Nazi's and the Bible was redefined to mean what the Nazi party wanted it to mean. Do we want this type of thing to happen in the United States because

Christians refuse to lower themselves to take action in the cesspool of politics?

It has already happened in the United States so we are not more morally correct than the German's that voted in the Nazi party. Blacks were held in slavery. Prejudice by some against other races continues to this day. Native Americans were persecuted, killed and treaties with them have been broken. Many ethnic groups and types of people have been discriminated against. Today on the internet and daily television newscasts, open general slurs and actual violence against law enforcement officers are allowed and condoned by many. Wearing a blue uniform should not allow people to freely commit violence against you.

My father-in-law was an ethnic minority, WWII veteran, a deputy sheriff in Milwaukee, and a Christian. I had the opportunity to talk with him extensively in the latter part of his life about his experiences. There may be unjust law enforcement officers but he was not one of them. I have confidence that the bulk of law enforcement officers in the United States at this time in history do not have a hidden agenda of hate. They are simply doing their job to the best of their ability. Improvements in training and better equipment are always desirable but they take tax dollars and time. Defunding the police instead of helping them to improve will lead to increased violence because criminals will take advantage of any weakness.

The current fad of condoning open hate speech against law enforcement by grouping all officers into a racist category should not be condoned by Christians of any ethnic group. It is just as dangerous as the sentiments about the Jews and others that led to the formation of Nazi power in Germany. I am not trying to reduce the horror of the atrocities committed against the Jews in WWII but extreme evil may grow from a small seed. The need for revenge against perceived injustice has led to violence and riots in our country from which no one is safe. There is nothing wrong with peacefully protesting and stating your opinion for a just cause but that is not all that is happening in the year 2020. Muzzling your opponent's speech is being accomplished by a variety of intimidation techniques including direct physical violence. MLK would not have approved of these tactics.

Christians need to speak up while they still can. The time is growing late. Standard Christian beliefs may eventually be labeled "hate speech" by the rule of law and no longer allowed to be presented in the public arena for everyone to consider. The teachings of the Bible will again be redefined by the state to help control the agenda of the allowed politically correct Christians just like the Nazi party did so long ago. Christians should not bow their knee or sacrifice their freedom to anyone but Christ. Christians have an obligation to God and their fellow human beings to take any reasonable action even politically, to promote truth and love towards all people.

Benefits of Christian Politics

Martin Luther King Jr said, "I believe that unarmed truth and unconditional love will have the final word in reality. This is why right, temporarily defeated, is stronger than evil triumphant." [2]

Christians will eventually overcome evil because they have truth and love on their side. Jesus is the source of that truth

[2] https://www.keepinspiring.me/martin-luther-king-jr-quotes/#:~:text=%E2%80%9CIf%20you%20can't%20fly,low%20as%20to%20hate%20him.%E2%80%9D

and love. Christians must follow his words to win any conflict with evil. MLK was killed but he still overcame and won his fight against racism. His weapons were God's word combined with the effect of nonviolent protest on the conscience of a nation. Some elements of the BLM protestors of 2020 would do well to remember how Dr. King won his battle and adapt his methods to their struggle before they create a lost cause out of the Black Lives Matters movement. Condoning violence because you hate a group of people is always wrong even if they wear blue. Even the police are innocent until proven guilty in a court of law.

My father only had an eighth-grade education and never traveled far from his home on a dairy farm where he was born but I am sure that he would realize that the violent elements of the BLM movement are incompatible with Christ just from watching television. Dodge County Wisconsin did not have many black people and I had always assumed he had not met many black people during his lifetime. I was wrong.

My father had worked closely with many black people during sugar beet harvesting, probably during World War II. It seemed to be customary at that time for the sugar beat workers to refer to each other by the N-word including calling my father the N-word in a non-derogatory manner.

When my father was old, I visited him at a large urban hospital for treatment and many black people were working on him. A black male nurse came into the room while I was there and my father referred to him with an N-word. I almost died of mortification right on the spot. I had never heard my father use the N-word before or negatively refer to black people in any way. I was petrified that the nurse would be offended. The nurse began joking crudely with my father and had been talking to him previously while I was gone. The nurse told me not to worry.

People like my father would be killed or injured by some elements of BLM just for being ignorant. Elements associated with BLM are not acting after the tradition of Martin Luther King Jr who valued nonviolent protest. MLK was a Christian and would not condone violent actions. I am willing to bet that MLK would have got along with my father after they talked for a while.

BLM is not being led by a Christian spirit and it is spawning violence without universally condemning it. MLK protested and his cause was triumphant in the final analysis without ever condoning violence. BLM does not clearly condemn violence. All of this shows that one of the great benefits of true Christianity in politics is nonviolence.

"Then Jesus said to him, "Put your sword back into its place! For all who take up the sword will die by the sword. Or do you think that I cannot call upon my Father, and he would put at my disposal at once more than twelve legions of angels?"
The Lexham English Bible (Mt 26:52–53)

Look at the movement that Jesus created during his brief time here on earth in the past. Jesus was only violent once while on earth to the best of my knowledge. During that incident, he was angry at those who cheated people attempting to worship God at the temple in Jerusalem by shortchanging their money and stealing from them. He never became violent over politics with the roman government even though it was oppressive. The body of Christ eventually became triumphant over the mighty roman empire's power using the words of Jesus and the testimony of his life.

Are Christians in the United States able to worship God and speak their minds with freedom? Having Christians like MLK involved in politics provides insurance that everyone can worship God according to their conscience and has the freedom to speak their mind publicly to anyone without fear of physical violence. True Christians are not perfect and they do not all agree with each other but they will not do violence to others. Self-preservation dictates that Christians take an active interest in political matters at this time in history.   MLK was killed for his actions and became a martyr for his cause. Not all Christians should need to be martyr's. Political action can be an excellent alternative to martyrdom.

COVID-19 has tested the first amendment to the Constitution of the United States. "Congress shall make no law respecting an establishment of religion, or **prohibiting the free exercise thereof; or abridging the freedom of speech**, or of the press; **or the right of the people peaceably to assemble, and to petition the Government for a redress of grievances."** [3] In 2020 peaceably assemble seems to be legal for certain chosen groups like BLM but the Church is forbidden to assemble. That's just not right. I believe that BLM should be allowed to peacefully assemble and that any Church should have the same right to assemble. The Church is being denied its constitutional rights under the first amendment and is being forced to stop

[3] First Amendment to the Constitution of the United States

the biblical practice of religion. The Church is being denied the following rights:

1. The free exercise of religion.
2. Freedom of speech,
3. Right to assemble.

The governor of one state denied the biblical right of singing in Churches. The apostle Paul was even able to sing in a roman prison 2000 years ago so we seem to have lost our rights since then. COVID-19 seems to confer extra rights on some groups and deny less desirable groups any rights.

"California pastor John MacArthur said in a sermon Sunday his church will continue to meet in-person despite a state-mandated ban on such gatherings, saying that Christ – not the state – is the "head of the church."
"I can't think of anything worse than to put an entire world into fear and then shut down the only place they could go to have their fear finally and completely removed," said MacArthur, a well-known author, and preacher at Grace Community Church in Sun Valley, Calif., whose sermons are syndicated on radio stations nationwide. "We're fulfilling our Lord's design." [4] While meetings at Church are banned,

---

[4] https://www.christianheadlines.com/contributors/michael-foust/john-

many authorities allow the essential work of bars and liquor stores to operate. Why do Christians vote for people who have contempt for their beliefs? People that make these biased decisions need to be voted out of office by Christians.

I think John MacArthur is right in his actions.

"And let us think about ⌊how to stir one another up to love⌋ and good works, not abandoning ⌊our meeting together⌋, as is the habit of some, but encouraging each other, and by so much more as you see the day drawing near." The Lexham English Bible (Heb 10:24–25)

Watching a video of a Church service is not the same as meeting together.

---

macarthurs-church-defies-order-to-close-we-must-obey-god-rather-than-men.html

Prejudice Against Christians In Politics

Some Christians tend to shoot themselves in the foot regarding involvement with politics. The Gospel message is not incompatible with publicly supporting good government policy or specific political candidates from a Christian perspective. Government policy is not as important as the Gospel message but government accommodation to Christian values will aid in the promotion of the Gospel. The policies in Saudi Arabia for example make the preaching of the Gospel difficult. In contrast, the United States enjoys relative freedom to preach the Gospel because of the first amendment to our Constitution.

I have talked to certain atheists that believe Christians should not be allowed to have any influence on public policy. After all the people who wrote our declaration of independence and constitution insisted on complete separation of Church and state. None of the founders of our country believed in the God of the Bible and they all were a bunch of white male slave owners anyways. Our modern experience allows us to interpret the laws with more humanistic values to achieve a better society.

Really? I think the opinions of many humanistic atheists regarding United States history and current public policy are a bunch of horse manure that they are using to promote their political agenda. The declaration of independence says that "We hold these truths to be self-evident, that all men are created equal, that they are endowed by their Creator with certain unalienable Rights, that among these are Life, Liberty and the pursuit of Happiness.--" [5] Most of the men who wrote the declaration of independence were strongly influenced by the Bible and Christian teaching. The evil of slavery existed at that time but we did fight the Civil War and many people died to correct that error.

---

[5] https://www.archives.gov/founding-docs/declaration-transcript

Some anti-Christian elements in our society are attempting to play a "long game" to eliminate Christian influence from our society by using the education system to brainwash potential voters. Young people go to certain colleges with atheist professors and are indoctrinated into anti-Christian beliefs. I went to Milwaukee School of Engineering in the 1980s and fortunately for me, it did not have a strong atheistic slant. God is real and engineers tend to mostly be pragmatic in my experience.

I did remember one humanities professor teaching a formal logic class who displayed some of his negative feelings towards Christianity. He said something about Christ and his disciples probably being traveling homosexuals. MSOE does not have tenure for its professors to the best of my knowledge but it did have a system of formal anonymous student reviews. In my review, I mentioned the logic professor's comments and suggested that he would benefit from sensitivity training for dealing with people of a different belief system than his world view. I also suggested that he was making inappropriate use of classroom time by discussing his personal beliefs during a class on formal logic. I probably didn't do much good with my review other than giving me personal satisfaction but there is always hope.

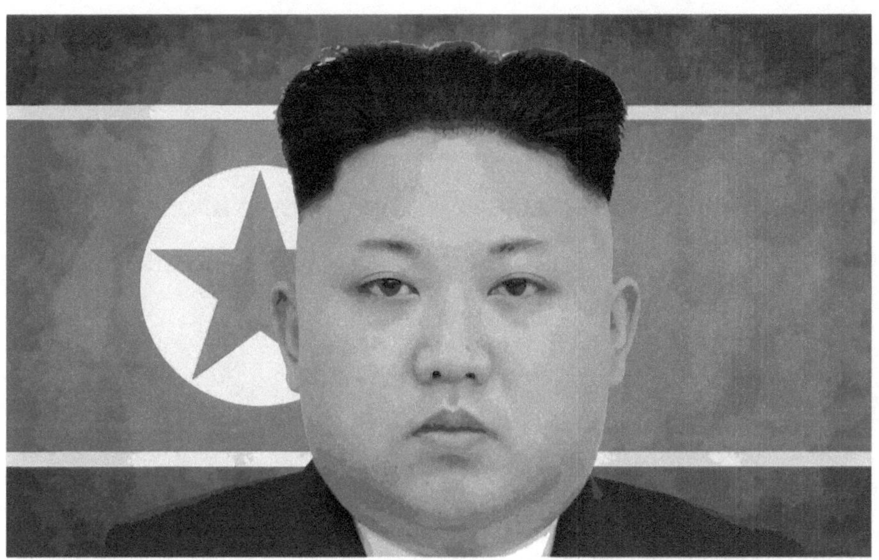

Alternatives to Christian Involvement in Politics

North Korea is a communist country that has made Christianity illegal. Anyone openly professing Christ is tortured or killed. Christians have no political influence of any kind. Would you want the United States to become more like North Korea? Communism appears to be a less than ideal choice for Christians or anyone who disagrees with it.

I have met brainwashed atheists in the United States who believe that Communism should be our goal. I asked them to show one example of where it has ever worked right. They replied that the whole world needs to accept communism under the control of the United Nations for it to work properly. They learned this enlightened knowledge from their educated professors in college.

"Claiming to be wise, they became fools,"
The Lexham English Bible (Ro 1:22)

Nazism subverted Christian beliefs using propaganda and allowed no dissenting political opinions from any minority group. The results were pure evil. Christians can't allow any political system that suppresses free speech to rule the country they live in. Free speech is essential for the transmission of the Gospel and the protection of minority groups. Violence to suppress free speech must be answered by whatever means necessary to stop it. Political action by Christians to advocate free speech rights is the least offensive action needed to oppose suppression of this basic human right.

Saudi Arabia is an Islamic country and Christians are not allowed to run for a government office to the best of my knowledge. "The Saudi Arabian Mutaween (Arabic: مطوعين), or Committee for the Promotion of Virtue and the Prevention of Vice (i.e., the religious police) prohibits the practice of any religion other than Islam.[8] Conversion of a Muslim to another religion is considered apostasy,[8] a crime punishable by death if the accused does not recant. There have been no confirmed reports of executions for either crime in modern times.[8] The Government does not permit non-Muslim clergy to enter the country for the purpose of conducting religious services."6 Do Christians want to allow Islamic law to rule countries they live in? I don't think that would be a good idea either.

To misquote Benjamin Franklin, If Christians don't all hang together then we will all hang separately. There are no viable alternatives to all Christians being involved in politics in the United States. Christians need to actively take a leading role in all public policy or those policies will be used as a weapon to eliminate the free exercise of our religion and destroy the fabric of our country. Christians need to control politics so that everyone is allowed the freedom to worship, talk, and believe as they determine is best for them

---

6
https://en.wikipedia.org/wiki/Christianity_in_Saudi_Arabia#:~:text=Accurate%20religious%20demographics%20are%20difficult,million%20Christians%20in%20Saudi%20Arabia.

and their children. Christians will lose their freedom in this country if we simply hide in our Churches and refuse to get our hands dirty with the political process.

Policy Changes Are Needed

The Bible often refers to Christians as sheep. Have you ever worked with real sheep because I have during my younger days? Our neighbor was a sheep owner and had a severe injury (probably from his sheep) so he serenely asked if I could load the sheep on a truck for transporting to a new location. Sheep didn't particularly impress me as a tough creature to deal with because I was used to Holstein dairy cows which are much bigger. Did you know that sheep will not follow you unless they know you? Check out the Bible (John 10) if you need proof.of their stubbornness.

My plan for loading my neighbor's sheep was to chase them into a long narrow passage and rope them one at a time to load them into the truck. Yeah, that plan didn't work out very well for me. I managed to chase them into a long narrow passage alright but when I tried to rope them they all simultaneously charged me. I caught the first one but the second one jumped over me and hit my shoulder knocking me to the ground. The rest of them trampled me into the ground and I still have a small scar on my leg from that experience. Eventually, I was able to rope them by separating them into several small individual pens. I am not sure where the truck was taking them.

Christians today are being chased into a passageway and being roped into going to a destination that may not be desirable. Politics, Media influence, Laws, and the Secular educational system are in the process of making it impossible for us to live in peace and effectively serve Christ. Christians need to start acting like sheep being threatened by someone they do not know.

The Johnson Amendment and any similar restrictions on free speech need to be cut out of the laws of the United States. "The Johnson Amendment is a provision in the U.S. tax code, since 1954, that prohibits all 501(c)(3) non-profit organizations from endorsing or opposing political candidates. Section 501(c)(3) organizations are the most common type of nonprofit organization in the United States, ranging from charitable foundations to universities and churches. The amendment is named for then-Senator Lyndon B. Johnson of Texas, who introduced it in a preliminary draft of the law in July 1954." (Wikipedia)

I have not seen anywhere in the Bible that God forbids his people from ever opposing specific secular government officials when they are attacking his people and their right to worship him. Moses specifically delivered Pharaoh a message from the Lord in person, "Let my people go." The problem today is that our rulers are listening to lies and lying to us. We do however need to have prayerful appropriate discretion when delivering our Christian message.

Taxing a Church can be used to destroy some functions of the Church because it could be taxed more than it could pay. This can't be allowed by Christians if possible. Churches should be allowed to criticize government officials and candidates by name because the actions of the government can be used to destroy Churches. Survival of Christianity requires governments to at least acquiesce to the biblical functions of the Church one way or another. God will make a way even in extreme circumstances but my personal preference would be for Christians to make their voice known before an evil political force controls their country and stop it from ever taking root. Nazism and Communism did not take over countries in a single day. It took time combined with a lack of coherent opposition.

Christians can still advocate for specific issues and educate the public even under the unbiblical restrictions of the Johnson amendment. I used to be in a Church that supplied voter education cards which listed specific issues cross-referenced to the response of the candidate on that issue. No attempt was made to endorse any specific candidate but the words of the candidates on each issue spoke for themselves. All Christian Churches should supply such information to their members and the public if possible.

Hate speech laws can be used to silence Christians with legal action because our speech is being defined as hate speech when convenient for those who oppose Christian values. Christians believe that the Holy Spirit has the power to transform a person from a sinner into a new creature in Christ by the power of the gospel. Suppose you can't tell someone the gospel because the government says it is hate

speech. Does that seem a little far fetched to you? Try telling children that the LGBTQ values are wrong in a public forum because it is a sin against Jesus. Today we have drag queens in public libraries reading sexually-oriented material
to little children and this is considered normal although COVID-19 has delayed some of these activities in 2020.

Prayer in public government schools is forbidden by law in the United States. Christians should not need to send their children to public schools because of financial considerations. Tax dollar vouchers should be used to reimburse parents for sending their children to Christian schools. All schools matter including Christian, public, and private. All types of schools should be funded by a total voucher system instead of simply wasting money on failing public schools. Allow parents to choose the school that their child attends. Inefficient schools would fail and efficient schools would gain more students. Large public schools are already becoming difficult to operate anyways because of COVID-19 so smaller private Christian schools are an obvious practical choice.

All types of education including public/private college should be funded by a total voucher system and the money should be supplied from taxes. Academic achievement should be the primary basis of determining which student is allowed to attend specific educational systems although other factors could carry some weight. A total voucher system would increase the diversity of thought in the educational system rather than having the current stranglehold by atheism.

Someone once told me that I should look at it as an opportunity when he fired me from my job. You know what, he was right. Getting fired from that job was probably the best thing that could have happened to me at that time. Christians need to avoid always looking at situations as just a problem and instead always think of everything as an opportunity to do God's work.

I
Voted

Action Plan for Christian Politics

Martin Luther King Jr. said, "We may have all come on different ships but we are in the same boat now." [7]

Right now Christians are in a sinking boat during a storm and we should all start praying for Jesus to calm the storm and help us get to the shore. We are more concerned about trivial things like sports and entertainment rather than the fact that Bibles and the symbols of our country are being burned.   Violent acts against innocent people are being committed in the street. There may come a day in the United States when we are not allowed to speak our mind or vote for the candidate of our choice. That day is not yet today but if we don't act together and vote our conscience it may be sooner than we think.

Major secular media sources such as CNN, FOX, NBC, ABC, and MSNBC have an anti-Christian bias in their editorial choices which spills over into their regular news coverage. Even Facebook and other secular social media outlets are in the beginning stages of censoring Christian political writing and speech. Christians should systematically

---

[7] https://www.keepinspiring.me/martin-luther-king-jr-quotes/#:~:text=%E2%80%9CIf%20you%20can't%20fly,low%20as%20to%20hate%20him.%E2%80%9D

use existing social media to get their values into the public arena when possible and develop independent media that is more accepting of their policy thinking.

Christians are becoming an outnumbered minority in the United States and they are fragmented politically into different groups because there are minor policy differences due to the teaching of different sects. There are also major areas of political agreement that could unite most Christian sects and also allow them to form coalitions with other political groups.

The current two major political parties are in the beginning stages of fragmentation in my opinion and the polls indicate that elections are balanced on a razor-thin margin. A unified voting faith coalition of people with Christian/Catholic/Jewish values could control the razor edge outcome of elections in the future. The existing two major political parties may someday cease to exist in their current form and that may not be the worst thing in the world.

A significant faith coalition political party could even deny the two major parties a plurality in the electoral college. The electoral college could then return to its early historic function of choosing a better president based on the electors votes. The "Tyranny of the majority" would be difficult for either major political party to achieve under these conditions. Trump or Biden? Maybe we can do better? Instead of faithless electors we should have faith filled electors.

Potential areas of agreement that could eventually form a faith coalition voting block may include:

1. Law and order
2. Repeal of the Johnson Amendment
3. Civil Rights
4. School Choice
5. Pro-Life
6. Family Values
7. Immigration Reform

The current violent intolerance against the police in our country can't be allowed forever or our society will cease to exist. The police can't be significantly defunded because mob rule incompatible with the free exercise of religion will result. Increased investment in the police along with additional training should be advocated instead of attempting to violently attack them. The increase in crime that will result from the current attempt to eliminate the police will make pro-law politics attractive to many people in the future.

The Johnson Amendment is unbiblical, unconstitutional, and should be repealed immediately. The Bible does not seem to forbid criticism of public officials/candidates by name or issue-oriented advocacy. An example:

"But Herod the tetrarch, who had been reproved by him concerning Herodias, his brother's wife, and concerning all the evil deeds that Herod had done, added this also to them all: he also locked up John in prison."
The Lexham English Bible (Lk 3:19–20).

 The first amendment says that Congress shall make no law prohibiting the free exercise of religion or abridging the freedom of speech. Please remember that John the Baptist was also executed for his public statements so you may also have to pay a price for expressing your opinion.

There is a time and place for political speech by Christians and it is not always necessary for Christians to stand on a soapbox ranting. At the same time, Christians pay taxes and we have a religious obligation to be good stewards of our money.

For because of this you also pay taxes, for the authorities are servants of God, busily engaged in this very thing. Pay to everyone what is owed: pay taxes to whom taxes are due; pay customs duties to whom customs duties are due; pay respect to whom respect is due; pay honor to whom honor is due.
The Lexham English Bible (Ro 13:5–7).

 In my opinion, our government officials and political candidates deserve the help of Christians in the form of a little constructive criticism. We do not owe political candidates respect when they call for funding abortion with our money, allowing riots to spread, cruelty against immigrants, or prejudice against the police.

MLK successfully protested against racial injustice and formed a powerful political movement using nonviolent methods. "As always, Christianity was a major theme in King's speech. He described a world in which people of many different backgrounds could work together, attend school together, and yes, pray together. He mentioned "God's children" on multiple occasions and expressed his hope that "the glory of the Lord shall be revealed, and all flesh shall see it together." However, he also shared his fervent desire that people of many backgrounds could band together in pursuing his dream: "Jews and Gentiles, Protestants and Catholics will be able to join hands and sing."[8] Civil rights and religious freedom are essential for any type of worthy Christian inspired political coalition.

School choice can become a successful political issue for Christians. The scourge of COVID-19 is changing the face of education because this terrible disease requires social distancing and that is not compatible with the old normal public school setting. Many public schools were already inefficient and failed to produce functional citizens. Christian schools are usually smaller and capable of adapting faster than public schools because they are not constrained by a bloated bureaucracy.   Christians should band together and set up hybrid Kindergarten through grade 12 schools that use a combination of online learning and in-person teaching.

All K-12 schools should be funded by vouchers paid for by the taxpayer. Parents should be able to choose where they want to send their children and use the voucher to pay for the school. It should make no difference whether the school is public or private. I believe parents will choose Christian schools if given the financial opportunity and that this choice

---

[8] https://www.geneva.edu/blog/uncategorized/mlk-dream-in-2019#:~:text=While%20most%20Americans%20are%20well,he%20was%20a%20devoted%20minister.

will be heavily favored in poor urban environments. The quality of education outcomes would be greatly enhanced by this plan. I believe that there is a constituency that would vote for a total voucher plan of this type if the benefits are clearly explained.

The Pro-Life movement already has a significant following and Pro-Life people would naturally be attracted to a political movement that advocated for its core belief. It is not possible to be a true Christian and be against life. An increase in the number of Christian schools that teach Pro-Life values will eventually result in more Pro-Life voters. Many immigrant voters already are Pro-Life and it may be possible to incorporate them into a political coalition.

Christians disagree with many of the beliefs of the LGBTQ community because they are incompatible with the Bible. Hatred or prejudice against LGBTQ people can never be condoned because Christ commands us to love all people as ourselves. The freedom to teach your children conservative family values is greater in a Christian school than in a public school. There is a current fad of LGBTQ legal attacks against Christian Businesses such as cake bakers. People who work at a Christian business would naturally gravitate towards a Christian political coalition that advocates family values and the freedom to work within your values.

Comprehensive immigration reform is an issue that should concern all Christians.

"And when an alien dwells with you in your land, you shall not oppress him. The alien who is dwelling with you shall be like a native among you, and you shall love him like yourself, because you were aliens in the land of Egypt; I am Yahweh your God."
The Lexham English Bible (Le 19:33–34).

Our country should have control over who enters the country and becomes a citizen. Criminals should not be allowed to immigrate here because they endanger everyone. The United States should grant controlled amnesty to undocumented aliens with a job already residing in this country. Legal immigration limits should be increased for anyone willing to get a job, serve in the military, or can contribute something positive to our society. That is how I interpret "Love them as yourself". Many immigrants would welcome a Christian political movement that directly helps them and supports family values. These types of immigrants would contribute votes to such a movement.

Christians may be able to learn something from modern Israeli politics. Small Israeli religious parties are sometimes able to form coalition governments with other parties that give them significant control of government policy on matters that are critical to their religion. Christians in the United States may consider building a coalition just like these small Israeli religious political parties.

The Republican and Democratic parties are both being weakened by extreme elements within their parties. Eventually, fragmentation of both parties may occur and groups of people may be cut loose from both parties that desire common sense and moral public policies from their politicians. Common sense seems to be somewhat lacking in the existing political leadership of both major parties.

Faith groups could attempt to politically unify with each other around common belief systems like the Moral Majority used to be but they probably won't have enough votes to be a dominant political force. An independent faith oriented political party may be able to form a coalition with disaffected people groups leftover from the weakened Republican/Democrat party fragmentation. This concept would take a significant amount of time to implement and it's a long shot. Sometimes a long shot is worth a try because you may hit your target.

Democrats believe that increased immigration from Mexico will increase their voter base because Hispanics seem to trend as Democratic voters. Democratic planning may backfire on them if Hispanics could be offered a faith coalition alternative that is more in line with Catholic values and does not have a tendency to racist sounding language like the Republican party. Many Hispanics are Catholic, Christian, Anti-abortion, and prefer family values. The Democratic party is taking Hispanic immigrants for granted and does not cater to their belief systems because the leadership believes that all immigrants will vote Democrat. The leadership may be wrong in the long run.

Christ is ultimately the final authority for Christians. Jesus told the twelve apostles:

"Behold, I am sending you out like sheep in the midst of wolves. Therefore be wise as serpents and innocent as doves."
The Lexham English Bible (Mt 10:16)

I believe that is good advice for all Christians today, especially any Christian involved in the political process. Christians can afford to play the "long game" because we know we will ultimately win a final victory.

About the Author

The short story is that I grew up on a Dairy farm in

Wisconsin, became a professional engineer, and married a

hot Sicilian babe from Milwaukee. My name is written in the

Lamb's Book of Life and my cat loves me. I have cancer that can't be removed surgically and other severe medical conditions but I am making my best effort to survive these issues and die of extreme old age.

I am an imperfect Christian, married with two children and a former Professional Engineer. Traveled around the United States and Canada for engineering work at dairy plants and pharmaceuticals. Grew up on a dairy farm with a large garden and fruit trees. I am a farm boy at heart trapped in the city by circumstance. I have Cancer, Crohn's disease, and other serious illnesses but I am not quite dead just yet.

I like Gardening, Glass Bottle Crafts, Science, Johnny Cash, Animals of all types, Collecting tools, Packers Football, and spending time with my family sometimes. I dislike riding in small planes, Cancer, filling out bureaucratic forms, and busybodies. I would be quite happy if I never had to travel again anywhere for any reason.

Graduated from Milwaukee School of Engineering. Worked at the Sellnow Dairy farm, Wurtz Specialty Ice, Lindberg Industrial Furnaces/Ovens, APV Crepaco (Dairy/Food/Nuclear), and Seiberling Associates (Dairy/Pharmaceutical).   The most entertaining engineering project that I ever worked on was at the Dannon Yogurt company in Ft. Worth, Texas.

Check out my other books on Amazon for additional enrichment.

The Family Farm Crisis Solution!

Glenn's Cancer Survival Guide

Glenn's Crohn's Disease Survival Guide

Keep an eye on my blog glennsellnow.wordpress.com for FREE stuff. I occasionally run a reduced price SALE of my books on Amazon.

Disclaimer

Although the author and publisher have made every effort to ensure that the information in this book was correct at press time, the author and publisher do not assume and hereby disclaim any liability to any party for any loss, damage, or disruption caused by errors or omissions, whether such errors or omissions result from negligence, accident, or any other cause.

This book describes my personal experiences. I have tried to recreate events, locales, and conversations from my memories of them. To maintain their anonymity in some instances, I have changed the names of individuals and places, I may have changed some identifying characteristics and details such as physical properties, occupations, and places of residence. Some of the material in this book may also be available in my blog postings and other books. No organization or individual has endorsed the ideas presented in this book unless specifically noted.

I am not a doctor and you should always consult a doctor about anything related to medicine or your health before any action is taken. This book is not intended as a substitute for the medical advice of physicians. The reader should regularly consult a physician in matters relating to his/her health and particularly concerning any symptoms that may require diagnosis or medical attention. I do not assume any liability for the use or misuse of the ideas contained I in this book.

Some quotes from the Bible in this book may be from the Lexham English Bible translation. It is a modern language version that has excellent study tools. Do not hesitate to compare this translation to the original Hebrew, Greek and Aramaic. Other English translations can also be consulted for clarity. I have not studied the original Hebrew, Greek, and Aramaic text. This makes me a poor Biblical student so take everything I say with a grain of salt and consult your local clergy with any questions.

No religious group endorses anything I write regarding the Bible. The Bible is inerrant in its original language and contains many types of literature that are difficult to interpret along with the simple Gospel that even a child can understand. I hope that I have not misinterpreted any Biblical passage but I can make mistakes because I am only human. If any quotes in this book have been taken out of context in your opinion just contact me at www.facebook.com/groups/sellnowupdate/ and I will take the appropriate corrective action.

Social Media Help

"Plans go wrong when there is no counsel,

but with many advisors it will succeed"

The Lexham English Bible (Pr 15:22).

My.bible.com is a website and app with many different standard translations of the Bible in English. The app will read the Bible to you. The creators of the website have probably never heard of my books and do not endorse them at all but I strongly recommend you take a look at this website/app. You can friend people on the website and communicate with them easily. (https://my.bible.com/bible)

Amazon.com/author/glennsellnow is where you can buy this book and other *Books*.

(http://amazon.com/author/glennsellnow)

Glennsellnow.wordpress.com has a lot of accurate information and excellent opinions that may help you or at least give you a chuckle if you need one.

(glennsellnow.wordpress.com)

Glenn's Book Updates is a Facebook group that gets insider information on my books. Anyone can join and discuss their opinion. The link to join is <u>Glenn's Book Updates</u> .

Good News

"that if you confess with your mouth "Jesus is Lord" and believe in your heart that God raised him from the dead, you will be saved."

Romans 10:9 LEB

Feedback and Reviews

Please leave feedback comments about this book on my

website (glennsellnow.wordpress.com) or on Amazon at my

author page amazon.com/author/glennsellnow. I am always

looking for ways to modify and improve my books. Your comments would be greatly appreciated and help me with that endeavor.   I may make periodic revisions to this book and future books under consideration based on your feedback.

If you have found this book useful or entertaining please leave a positive review at amazon.com/author/glennsellnow. You may also leave a comment on any subject at my blog glennsellnow.wordpress.com by using the contact form on the site or simply leaving a comment on any post.

God Bless you and thanks for reading my book!